LOVE IS BUBBLEGUM

by Kailyn Lowry

with illustrations by Fuuji Takashi

A POST HILL PRESS BOOK
ISBN (Hardcover): 978-1-61868-860-6
ISBN (eBook): 978-1-61868-861-3

LOVE IS BUBBLEGUM
(C) 2015 by Kailyn Lowry
Artwork (C) 2015 by Post Hill Press
All Rights Reserved
Illustrations by Fuuji Takashi

Post Hill Press
275 Madison Avenue, 14th Floor
New York, NY 10016
http://posthillpress.com

Printed in Canada

Dedicated to my boys, Isaac and Lincoln. You are my heart.

Love comes in many forms, shapes and sizes. We can love things, places and people. Sometimes, we can feel and show love without saying it.

"Love looks like a heart, or bubblegum."

- Paige, age 4

...people who support each other."

– Rylee, age 7

"Love is when someone protects and cares about you."

- Alex, age 8

"Your heart helps you give love and love is a really good thing."

- Claire, age 4

"...I know I love something when it looks and smells yummy."

— Katelyn, age 4

"Love is my mom and sisters reading me books before bed."

- Piper, age 4

"Love makes you feel happy because everyone you love is caring about you."

- Mia, age 7

"Love feels like eating an ice cream cone."

- Colton, age 5

"I love giraffes."
- Sophie, age 5

Love is many different things.
Love is caring and it's very special.
Most importantly, love is... love.

THE END